MW00522812

who knew?

Beauty
on a Budget

Money-Saving Solutions and Everyday Remedies

Jeanne Bossolina-Lubin AND *Bruce Lubin*

CASTLE POINT
PUBLISHING

Cover and interior design by Lynne Yeamans

Castle Point Publishing
58 Ninth Street
Hoboken, NJ 07030
www.castlepointpub.com

ISBN: 978-0-9832376-4-8

Printed and bound in the United States of America

2 4 6 8 10 9 7 5 3 1

Please visit us online at www.WhoKnewTips.com

Table of Contents

Introduction

We've all been there: Standing in the cosmetics section of a drugstore, holding a product that promises everything we've ever wanted, and thought, "Do I really need to spend this much money?" The answer, of course, is "no," and with hundreds of tips on the following pages you'll find out why: beauty products you can make yourself at home, easy ways to extend the life of your cosmetics, ways to wear your wardrobe to its fullest potential, and homemade remedies and first aid for a plethora of ailments (hey, we had to give Bruce a section to write in this book!).

Whether you want to make homemade face masks, clean your jewelry with materials you already have around your house, keep the static cling out of your skirt, heal a canker sore the all-natural way, get your hair looking beautiful, or just keep your shoes from stinking, you'll find it (and much more) here.

Jeanne and Bruce

Chapter One

Face & Body

The 30-Second Skin Reviver

Whether you just need to wake up, or freshen up your skin, here's the perfect 30-second skin reviver. Place a fresh hand towel under steaming hot water (not boiling—the hottest you get out of your tap is fine), then cover your entire face with it for 30 seconds. Then use the towel or a warm, wet washcloth to buff your T-zone area (chin, nose, and forehead). For a finishing touch, splash cold water all over your face to leave your pores tight and tingling.

C the Difference

Everyone knows that vitamin C is a miracle immune booster, but it works great as a facial cleanser too. Pick up those vitamin C drink powders in any grocery store for super-cheap. Mix ¼ package with 1 tablespoon water. Scrub onto your skin, leave to dry, then rinse. The vitamin helps your skin cells produce more collagen—that highly coveted protein some people pay top dollar for.

Beware of Overdoing It

Over-cleansing is a major cause of sensitive skin, as it strips the skin's underlying layers of its natural protective properties. Make sure you use a cleanser that's right for your skin type and don't wash your face too often—if you notice red spots or rough patches, cleanse less regularly or try applying a moisturizer afterward.

Scrub Away from the Face!

Don't be tempted to use a body scrub on the delicate skin of your face. Body scrubs contain larger, rougher granules than facial exfoliants, and they'll irritate and inflame the sensitive skin on your face.

Got Exfoliant?

Looking for a fabulous age-defying skin treatment? Check your fridge! Milk is nutritious for your insides *and* your outsides: Lactic acid works as an exfoliant, and milk's amino acids and proteins have a calming effect on red skin. Just dab onto skin with a clean cloth. Stick to fat-free milk for the best results.

Brighten Skin Naturally

Rubbing a slice of pineapple or papaya onto your skin will help remove dead skin cells. Leave for five minutes, then rinse off with water. These fruits contain the papain enzyme, a natural, nonabrasive botanical that dissolves dead skin cells, which makes it a great ingredient for face masks and exfoliations. It deeply cleanses without stripping, leaving dull skin smoother and more refined.

Drink Up

Drinking red wine is good for the heart because it contains antioxidants such as resveratrol, which strengthens blood vessels and prevents blood clots. But red wine is also great for your skin! Add some to any hydrating face mask and the antioxidants will lend powerful anti-aging properties to the treatment.

Not Just for Baking

Check your pantry for even more natural skincare elixirs. Large-granule sugar is an excellent exfoliant that can be mixed with any regular cleanser. Try brown sugar, if you have it: It's not as processed as white sugar. Consider stirring in a bit of olive oil, which has wonderful moisturizing and anti-inflammatory properties.

The Truth About Moisturizers

If you're looking for a way to cut back on cosmetics, the first place to start is with your moisturizer. Whether it's night cream, day cream, anti-aging lotion, or anti-wrinkle solution, it's all pretty much the same. Pick a moisturizer with an SPF of at least 15—other than that, go with a less expensive brand whose smell you like. Your wallet will know the difference, but your face never will.

Time to Wake Up!

In the morning, your face can look pale and puffy because of the natural nocturnal slow-down in the body. When putting on your moisturizer, take the opportunity to gently massage all the muscles in your face to waken up the lymphatic system and jump start the circulation.

A Work-Out for Your Face

To tighten a wobbly chin area, push your lips tightly together and make a wide grimace to contract your lower facial muscles. Hold for three seconds and repeat 20 times each day.

Our Five Favorite
Homemade
Face Masks

1. GO BANANAS
Bananas are great for oily skin. Mash one banana with a teaspoon of honey and a couple of drops of lemon juice. Apply to your face and let sit for 15 minutes before washing with a cool washcloth.

2. SOLUTION FOR DRY SKIN
Mix one egg yolk with a teaspoon of honey and a teaspoon of olive oil. Leave on your face for as long as possible, then wash off. The vitamin A in the egg yolk is great for your skin!

3. TASTES GREAT, TOO!
Mix ¼ cup brown sugar with 1½ tablespoon whole or 2 percent milk. Rub into your face, then leave on for 10 minutes. The brown sugar will exfoliate while the milk will moisturize.

4. YOU WON'T BELIEVE IT TILL YOU TRY IT
Clay cat litter is actually the exact same clay that's found in some of the most expensive face masks on the market. Find some cat litter labeled "100 percent all-natural clay" and mix it with water until it gets to the consistency you want. Adding a couple drops of scented oil will also help make it seem less like you're applying cat litter to your face. Wash the mask off after it hardens.

5. SKIN SOOTHER
This face mask is perfect for sunburned or irritated skin. Combine _ cup full-fat yogurt with 2 tablespoons oatmeal. Mix vigorously for one minute, then apply to your face. Leave on for at least 10 minutes, then wash off with warm water.

Natural Toner

Toner is a final layer of beauty product to use after cleaning your skin. It will help you get a fresh look, reduce puffiness, and tighten your pores. To make your own all-natural version, combine a quarter of a cucumber (no need to peel) with 1½ tablespoons witch hazel and 1 tablespoon water (distilled if you have it) in a blender. Add a little lemon juice and blend until smooth (which should only take a minute). Push through a mesh tea strainer and throw out the solids. Store the toner in the fridge, and when you're ready to use it, dab on your face with a cotton pad or ball. It can be used daily and should last a few weeks. Enjoy! Once you try it you'll never go back to the store-bought kind.

Breakfast Beauty Treatment

Here's another great recipe for a homemade toner to apply to your face after washing: Combine a peeled kiwifruit with 1½ teaspoons lime juice in a blender and blend until smooth. Apply to a small amount to skin and let dry. Keep remaining mixture in the fridge in a sealable container for one to two weeks. You'll love the smell almost as much as how great it makes your skin feel!

—AUDREY PASQUERELLI, RALEIGH, NC

Another Yummy Toner

Here's super easy homemade toner that shrinks pores and leaves your skin clean and smooth: Mix ¼ cup tomato juice and ¼ cup watermelon juice. You can store for roughly three days in the fridge.

Give Your Skin a Feast

Skin is the last organ to get the benefits of the good things you eat, so often there's precious little nutrients left, even if your diet is fantastic. To make sure your skin gets the nourishment it needs, choose face treatments that are high in such essential minerals as calcium, magnesium, and zinc to give it a boost.

Get Smooth with Soy

Soy proteins can help make skin temporarily smoother by improving firmness and elasticity if applied regularly. Look for them as ingredients in new "high-tech" face creams.

A Cream You Can't Live Without

Available online and in health food and vitamin shops, horse chestnut cream is said to diminish the tiny red veins that appear on your cheeks and nose as you age. Skin becomes thinner and loses some of its collagen as you get older, and horse chestnut cream improves blood circulation and will make these annoying veins disappear.

Take a Deep Breath

Make your nighttime lotion regimen even more effective by taking five deep breaths to boost levels of oxygen to the skin before smoothing on your cream.

Overnight Hydration

During the night, the skin rests and repairs itself after the stresses of the day, so nothing's worse than waking up to dry skin in the winter. Use a humidifier or place a damp towel over your radiator at night to replenish moisture in the air and keep your skin hydrated. This helps to humidify the air around you, and reduces excessive water loss from your skin.

Simple Beauty Treatment

Here's a great addition to your nighttime beauty regime that is simple to do, and feels luxurious! Before washing your face, simply wet a washcloth with hot water, then wring out and place over your face for 30–60 minutes, refreshing with more hot water as needed. The warmth will help open up your pores, allowing your cleanser to reach the deepest bits of dirt, and making your face feel even cleaner.

—MANDY MELLETT, CHEYENNE, WY

Goodbye to Puffy Eyes

To combat puffy eyes, place slices of cucumber on them. It may seem like an old wives' tale, but cucumbers have a mild anti-inflammatory action. To make your experience even more enjoyable, keep the cucumber in the fridge until you're ready to use it. The coolness will feel wonderful on your eyelids, and the cold will help further restrict blood vessels, making puffiness go down.

Our Five Favorite
Acne Busters

1. RAW POTATO

Sprouting pimples like they're going out of style? Try this neat trick to clear up your face. Cut a raw potato in half and rub the flat end over your face. Leave the juice on for 20 minutes before rinsing off. The starch in the potato will help dry out your oily skin.

2. DIAPER RASH CREAM

Dab a bit of diaper rash cream on offending areas, and the zinc oxide in the cream will dry up oil and kill bacteria, while the moisturizers making your skin as soft as a baby's behind.

3. ICE CUBE

If a giant pimple sprouts up at work, here's a way to make it less noticeable without applying a face mask (or diaper rash cream!) at your desk: Place an ice cube on it for 30–60 seconds, then place a few eye drops onto a tissue and hold it on the spot for 3 minutes. This will cause the blood vessels below your skin to contract, making the pimple less red and easing some of the irritation.

4. ASPIRIN

A topical paste made out of water and crushed-up aspirin will help get rid of pimples. Wash your face with warm water first, apply the paste, then rinse off with cool water after 10 minutes. This treatment should not be used more than five days in a row as it can dry out your skin.

5. DIET

You know you're supposed to get plenty of omega-3 fatty acids, but you may not know they help reduce acne. So to stop break-outs, break out the walnuts, fish (especially salmon), flax seed, soybeans, cauliflower, and cabbage. But before you indulge, be aware that food allergies can actually cause acne, so ask your doctor to test you for food allergies if acne is a problem.

Herbal Eye Treatment

Reduce puffy or swollen eyes with a green tea compress. Dip a cotton swab into the green tea, drain off excess moisture, and then dab gently around the eye area. This will help to tighten the skin around the eyes.

More Tricks for Puffy Eyes

Fix a puffy under-eye area by rubbing egg whites on it. As the egg whites dry, you'll feel the skin get tighter. Leave on for a few minutes after it dries, then rinse off with cool water. Or soak cotton pads in a solution of ½ teaspoon salt and 1 cup hot water, then apply them to your eyes and relax. Your eyes will be less puffy in 15 minutes or less.

The Spoon Solution

If all else has failed in your efforts to de-puff your eyes, try frozen spoons. Put two spoons in the freezer for five minutes, then roll them slowly back and forth over your eyes until you feel them start to warm up. Make sure your skin is completely dry before you do this, or you'll be faced with a new problem entirely.

For Luscious Lips

The best remedy for chapped lips? Buy a child's toothbrush with a really soft head, dip it in Vaseline, and scrub the heck out of your lips. It will get rid of rough patches while moisturizing the rest.

—AMY FORSTADT, HIGHLAND PARK, IL

Spider Veins Be Gone!

Here's an easy way to help prevent those annoying spider veins on your legs. Several times a day, roll onto the balls of your feet and then your tiptoes from a standing position. Hold for a few seconds and repeat a few times. This will keep the blood flowing in your legs and prevent spider veins from forming.

—JOAN TURNER, ANNISTON, AL

Hide Your Tan, Don't Tan Your Hide

Uh-oh, you got a little carried away with the fake tanner, and you need a quick fix! If unevenness of color is the problem, try gently rubbing the area with baking soda on a damp sponge. If you simply used too much tanner, wet a cotton ball with alcohol and rub it over your skin. You can also try using bleach made for body hair.

Keep Your Razor Sharp

Shaving with a dull razor can lead to razor burn and in-grown hairs, so be sure your razor is always sharp. The easiest way? Store it head-down in some olive oil. Rust is actually the culprit when it comes to dull razors, and the olive oil makes a protective seal that keeps water out. Bonus: It will help moisturize your skin!

Close Shave

Instead of buying expensive shaving creams or foams, try shaving with hair conditioner. (Buy the cheapest kind.) The conditioner will soften the hair and provide a layer of protection between your blade and your skin. You'll even find your shave is closer.

Vanquish Ingrown Hairs

Suffering from in-grown hairs? Here's an all-natural solution that will ease the itch and pain. Combine 1 cup sugar, the juice from half a lemon, 2 teaspoons apple cider vinegar, and ¼ cup honey. Blend it together until smooth, then heat in the microwave until warm (about 15–20 seconds). Let sit on the affected area for twenty minutes.

Sweet as Honey

Soft, supple skin is as easy as using a little honey. Simply apply honey straight from the jar on to skin that has been moistened with warm water. Leave for up to 30 minutes, then rinse off.

Get Rid of Dead Skin

Another way to slough off dead skin easily is by applying mayonnaise over any dry, rough patches. Let sit for 10 minutes, then wipe away with a washcloth that has been dampened with warm water.

Love the Gloves

Once a month, cover your hands in petroleum jelly or thick hand cream, and slip them into some soft cotton gloves for the night. In the morning, all the cream will have been absorbed, leaving you with the smoothest, softest hands you've ever had. You can also soften your feet the same way (just use socks rather than gloves).

Our Five Favorite
Sunburn Solutions

1. AN APPLE A DAY

Nothing's worse than a bad sunburn. The good news is you don't need an expensive lotion to soothe your poor, burnt skin. Just cut an apple in half, remove the core, and rub over the affected area for 3–4 minutes. Apples will keep your skin from blistering or peeling.

2. VINEGAR TO THE RESCUE AGAIN

To help ease the pain of a sunburn, rub vinegar on the affected area with a cotton ball or soft cloth. You may smell a bit like salad dressing, but your skin will immediately feel cooler.

3. DON'T HOLD THE MAYO

We all know of aloe's healing properties for sunburn, but when you don't have any on-hand, mayonnaise is a great stand-in (yes, mayonnaise!). Just make sure you're out of the sun before you apply it.

4. STARCHY RELIEF

Starch is fantastic at easing sunburn pain. If someone in your family has a sunburn and you're making pasta or potatoes, save the water you boiled them in and let it cool. Then rub the water onto sunburned areas for some immediate relief.

5. AFTER-SUN TEA

Green tea is another option for treating sunburns. Use a washcloth soaked in tea that has been cooled in the refrigerator as a compress on your tender skin. (Some people say topically applied green tea may even protect against skin cancer.) This is also a great way to ease a sunburned scalp. After washing and rinsing your hair as usual, pour the cooled tea over your scalp. Your skin will thank you!

Moisturize Before You Get Dirty

Slather on a heavy layer of hand moisturizer before painting or doing other dirty chores. It will prevent dirt and paint from seeping into your skin, making clean-up easier. White soap under your nails will help, too.

Give Your Hands a Break

Because the skin on your hands is thin and endlessly ravaged by the elements, keep them as dry as much as possible—never walk out of a restroom with wet hands. Water left on hands will evaporate, which will dry them out and can even cause them to turn red. If you're especially prone to dry hands, look for a hand cream that contains lanolin.

Instant Hand Sanitizer

To avoid spending money on expensive hand sanitizers, make your own at home with these ingredients: 2 cups aloe vera gel, 2 teaspoons rubbing alcohol, 4 teaspoons vegetable glycerin, and 15 drops eucalyptus oil. Mix the ingredients well and you should be able to use it the same way you'd use the commercially made version.

Rosemary Rejuvenation

If it's the end of the long day, help your achy feet with some rosemary. Fill a bucket or footbath with warm water, and add several rosemary sprigs. They'll relax and cool your feet in minutes!

—Hailey Ranaudo, Washington, DC

Feet Freshener

Smelly feet? To easily freshen them, simply rub a few slices of lemon over each foot. It will also help prevent athlete's foot.

Foot Bath for Health

If you find that you're susceptible to athlete's foot, here's a trick that will keep that nasty fungus at bay. Once or twice a week, soak your feet in a hot bath with two cloves of crushed garlic mixed in. The garlic will kill athlete's foot before it starts, and you won't be afraid to walk around in sandals. To treat a case of athlete's foot that has already begun, try soaking your toes in mouthwash. It may sting a little, but the nasty fungus will be gone in just a few days.

Foot Bath Formula

If you need a good soak in a foot bath, here's a soothing recipe to use. Pour a gallon of water into whatever container you use for foot soaking, and then add 1 cup lemon juice, 1 tablespoon olive oil, and ¼ cup milk. Mix thoroughly, stick your feet in, and relax!

Treatment for Tired Feet

To rejuvenate tired feet, pamper them with this home spa treatment. Massage some butter into your soles, then wrap your feet in warm, moist towels and let sit for 10 minutes. When you unwrap them they may smell a little like popcorn, but they'll be soft and feel great.

Drunken Fungus

Battling toenail fungus? Soak your toes in the darkest beer you can find. The yeast in the beer attracts the fungus out from underneath your nails. (Unfortunately, it's important that you don't *drink* any beer during this treatment! It will up the yeast content in your body, making the toenail fungus more likely to stick around.)

Soften Rough Feet

For the softest feet you've ever experienced, try this before-bed routine: Rub down your feet with vegetable oil, then put on some old socks. When you wake up, the oil will be gone and your feet will be super soft.

Homemade Bath Pillow

To make your own bath pillow, reuse a household item no one seems to be able to get rid of: packing peanuts! Pour packing peanuts into a large, resealable freezer bag, then let out some of the air and seal. Place in the bath as a soft resting place for your head.

A Luxurious Bath Treat

You can literally bathe in your favorite perfume by making your own scented bath oil. Just add a few drops of perfume to a quart of baby oil, shake well, and add to your bath.

Homemade Bubble Bath

You don't need expensive bath gels to get a luxurious bubble bath. To make your own bubble bath, simply place soap slivers in a mesh drawstring bag. (To get soap slivers, use a vegetable peeler on a sturdy bar of soap.) Attach the bag to the tap while the water is running. For even more fragrance, put a couple of drops of favorite essential oil in the bag, or herbs like rosemary and thyme.

The Best Bath

Make your bath time work for you by adding Epsom salts to the water. Epsom salts are made from the mineral magnesium sulfate, which draws toxins from the body, sedates the nervous system, and relaxes tired muscles. Goodbye expensive bath salts!

Flowery Bath Oil

For an inexpensive, luxuriously fragrant bath oil, mix sunflower oil with either crushed lavender or rose petals (or both). Let it stand for a few days before using it.

Helping Oatmeal Help You

Have you ever noticed that oatmeal is often the main ingredient in bath products? Well guess what—you have that very same oatmeal in your kitchen! Unfortunately, it's not as easy as just throwing some into a hot bath. First, grind the oatmeal down in a blender or coffee grinder to expose its inner skin-soothing qualities. Then place it in a piece of cheesecloth with a few drops of your favorite scented oil. While you're running your bath, hold it under the faucet, or tie it with a bit of string. You'll have a luxurious oatmeal bath, and even a little sachet you can use as a washcloth to help you exfoliate your skin.

A Little Lemon in Your Bath

You've finally found a few secret minutes to have a relaxing bath! Supercharge it by adding some lemon or apple juice. They're natural exfoliants, so they'll help get rid of dry skin. They'll also make the water smell wonderful!

Chapter Two

Hair Care Hints

Time for a Head Massage

It turns out that the person washing your hair at the salon is onto something! When you apply shampoo or conditioner, take a few moments to give yourself a slow fingertip scalp massage. Using gentle circular motions and a reasonable amount of pressure pushing down onto the scalp, you will boost blood circulation around the follicles and stimulate re-growth. Similarly, if you want to strengthen your hair, make sure to brush or comb it thoroughly each night. This will increase circulation in your scalp, loosen dry skin, and help moisturize your hair with your body's natural oils.

Cold Shine

Extra-shiny hair starts in the shower! Finish your final rinse with a blast of the most freezing cold water you can bear. It closes the hair cuticles so that light bounces off them, resulting in super-shiny locks.

Get Rid of Greasy Hair

Vinegar is not just for the kitchen: It's an effective degreaser for oily hair! Simply shampoo your hair as usual, rinse, then pour ¼ cup vinegar over it and rinse again.

Hand-Brewed Shampoo

It may surprise you to discover that beer has practical uses other than guzzling, but it's true. One of the best ones is enlivening flat hair. Mix three tablespoons of your favorite brew with half a cup of warm water, and after shampooing, rub the beer solution into your hair. Let it sit awhile before rinsing it off, and your hair will get that lively bounce back.

Too Much Hair Product?

If your hair is starting to feel filmy, blend ¼ teaspoon baking soda into your normal amount of shampoo, then wash as usual. The baking soda will remove the filmy feeling from your hair.

—MARCIA LUBIN, EDINA, MN

Hair Buzz

Here's another defense of caffeine: It helps your hair grow in thicker. One day, a topically applied shampoo containing caffeine may cure hair loss. For now, go for the kind you drink, especially coffee or black or green tea, and pour it over your hair before shampooing.

Our Five Favorite
Ways to Eliminate Dandruff

1. ASPIRIN

Aspirin can help reduce dandruff, but perhaps not in the way you might think. Crush a couple of tablets and add them to your normal shampoo. Then wash your hair as usual, letting the shampoo sit on your hair for 1–2 minutes before washing out.

2. LEMON JUICE

Did you know that dandruff is caused by bacteria clogging up your hair follicles? You can fight this bacteria with a little lemon juice! Squeeze the juice from one lemon and add ½ cup warm water, then pour over your scalp and let sit for five minutes before shampooing as usual.

3. DIET

Dandruff got you down? Try decreasing it by making some changes to your diet. Increase your intake of raw foods that are high in enzymes (fruit, vegetables, and nuts), and if it still doesn't improve, try swallowing two spoonfuls of flax seed oil a day.

4. THYME

If your scalp is getting flaky, try treating it with a mixture of 2 tablespoons dried thyme and 1 cup water. Let the water boil, then add the thyme and wait 5 minutes. Remove from the heat and let cool, then strain out the thyme and pour the water on your hair and scalp after you've washed and rinsed it. To let it work, don't rinse it out for 12 hours—but don't worry, your hair will dry fine (and smell delicious)!

5. SALT

Here's a quick fix to stop dandruff in its tracks. Just rub 2 table-spoons of salt into your scalp before shampooing and watch those flakes become a thing of the past.

Break Down Build-Up

Using styling products can make your hair look limp since shampoos don't always take care of the build-up. Every other week mix ¼ cup of baking soda with enough water to create a paste. In the shower, rub the paste into your hair, rinse, and then wash and condition as you would normally. The baking soda takes care of all of the hair product build-up and there's no need to buy any sort of expensive special shampoos.

—Jennifer Starkey, Webster Groves, MO

Help Dry Hair

Suffering from dry hair? Here's a surefire way to make your hair moist again. Mash a banana and mix with a teaspoon of almond or olive oil. Rub the mixture into your hair and scalp, and let sit for 20 minutes. Rinse off and shampoo and condition as usual. You'll be surprised at the results!

Hot Oil Treatment at Home

Instead of paying a salon to do it, give yourself a hot oil treatment at home for cheap. Rinse your hair completely with very hot water, then rub a tablespoon of baby oil into the hot hair—for longer hair, use more oil. Put your hair in a towel and wait at least 30 minutes; then wash as usual to get the oil out.

Delicious Hair Mask

For a deep-conditioning hair mask, mash the meat of an avocado with 1 cup mayonnaise. Rub it into your hair and cover your head with plastic wrap or with a shower cap. After twenty minutes, wash it out with your usual shampoo.

Easy Tip for the Shiniest Hair

Don't toss out that last bit of hair conditioner with the bottle! Instead, make it into a luxurious leave-in conditioner by adding 3 tablespoons of water and shaking. Put into a spray bottle to spray over wet hair after showering, and your locks will never be shinier!

—JESSICA HOLGATE, ATLANTA, GA

Hot Honey Hair

Give your hair and scalp a treat with an organic conditioner made from honey and olive oil. Mix equal parts together and warm in the microwave. Then apply the mixture to clean, towel-dried hair, and wrap in a warm towel for 20 minutes before washing out. Your hair will be smooth, shiny, and ultra-soft.

Your Hair Won't Know the Difference!

For a cheap alternative to hair gel, try a light hand lotion instead. Especially if you have a short cut, it works great to weigh down curls and frizzies, and costs less than half the price. Hand lotion is also great as a hair product because you can find it in so many scents—you'll probably find one you like even more than your normal hair-care product!

Deter Hair Dye

When dying clients' hair, I use this tip when they want to catch up on *Cosmo* but can't read without their glasses! Just cover the arms of the glasses in foil and you'll make sure none of the strong hair dye gets on them.

—SHEILA H., CARLISLE, PA

Go Blonde

If you have brown or dark blonde hair, you can add highlights without chemicals and without hardly any cost. First cut a lemon into quarters or eighths, then cut a slit in the middle, as if you were going to put the wedge on the rim of a glass. Wash your hair as usual, and while it's still wet, place a strand of your hair in the slit, beginning at your scalp and running the wedge down to the tips of your hair. Sit outside in direct sunlight until your hair dries, all you'll have lovely blonde streaks. Repeat in one week to make the streaks even brighter.

Dyeing To Change Your Hair?

Uh-oh, you just tried dying your hair a new color, and it looks bad enough that you don't want to leave the house without a hat. Instead of washing your hair 20 times to lessen the effects of the dye, just wash it three or four times using an anti-dandruff shampoo that contains zinc pyrithione. This chemical diminishes dye more quickly without damaging your hair.

—SHANICE JOHNSON, PAMPA, TX

Kitchen Color Corrector

If your blonde hair turns a strange shade of green after a summer spent swimming in chlorinated pools, comb tomato ketchup through your hair and leave it on for 20 minutes to neutralize the color. (This is a fantastic way to use up those packets stockpiled from fast-food places.) Wash and condition as usual and your hair will be a beautiful blonde again! Alternatively, you can rub cider vinegar into your hair *before* jumping in the water, which helps prevent color change.

Another Cure for Chlorinated Hair

If your hair has changed color from too much chlorine, here's another way to fix it. Crush 10 aspirin tablets into a cup of warm water, then work the solution through your hair. Let it sit for about 15 minutes, then wash out, and your hair should be back to its old self.

Summer Scalp

Hot summer sunshine can increase sweat production and make your scalp look and feel much greasier. To counteract this problem, try more frequent washings with a small amount of shampoo, and use a much lighter conditioner than you use in the winter.

Protect Your Hair From Beach Damage

Spending a windy summer day out on the beach? Strong winds on a sandy beach can cause as much damage to your hair as the sun, so to protect your locks run some leave-in conditioner into your hair before you go. Choose one that contains vitamin B5, which will nourish and protect your hair.

Cornstarch Gets Results

If you don't have time for a shower, use cornstarch or baking soda to get quickly the dirt and grease out of your hair. Shake a little where your hair is parted, let it sit for a minute or two, then flip your head upside-down and massage it out.

Hair Freshener

A dryer sheet can freshen up your hair when it's full of smoke or when you haven't had time to wash it. Keep one tucked into your purse at all times, and rub on your hair when needed. (As a bonus, it will help tame frizzy, dry hair.)

Our Five Favorite
Tips for Taming Curly Hair

1. BE COLD
After shampooing and conditioning, rinsing your hair with the coldest water you can stand can help cut back on frizziness.

2. HANDS-ON
As counterintuitive as it might seem, combs and brushes are a no-no with curly hair, because their close-together bristles separate hair strands and can make a curl into a frizz ball! Instead, use your fingers or a comb whose bristles are spaced far apart.

3. DIFFUSE THE SITUATION
With curly hair, it's usually better to air dry it, but if you're using a hair dryer, use a diffuser attachment. It will minimize heat damage and keep your curls from separating.

4. STYLING MUST-HAVE
Dilute your favorite conditioner with water until it's runny, then add to a spray bottle and use in the morning when trying to tame your locks.

5. FRIZZINESS BUSTER
Use this treatment to moisturize your locks and keep frizzies at bay: Mix together 1 egg yolk and 2 tablespoon olive oil (double the recipe if you have longer hair). Rub over your hair and place a shower cap on top, then leave in for 15–30 minutes before rinsing out. You won't believe how smooth and silky you hair becomes!

Don't Tear Your Hair

When hair is damp or wet it is much weaker and more easily damaged. Always treat wet hair carefully, and use a wide-toothed comb to straighten out tangles rather than a brush, which can create split ends.

Hair Today, Gone Tomorrow

To get your combs and hairbrushes completely clean of hair spray and other hair products, soak them in warm water with either two dryer sheets or a couple tablespoons of liquid fabric softener. Let sit for 2–3 hours, then simply rinse under the faucet. Alternately, you can soak them in a mixture of 1 quart hot water and 2 tablespoons baking soda for an hour. Rinse and enjoy your like-new brushes!

Tips for Thin Hair

Hair naturally thins out as part of the aging process, as the number of follicles capable of growing hairs gradually declines. A straight part with hair that just hangs down from it will emphasize the problem, so ask your stylist to create a style that incorporates color and texture.

Is Your Look Working for You?

Many women (and some men) love having long locks, but a thick, solid curtain of glossy hair can overwhelm your face and make your skin look dull and tired. If you have long hair, make sure to cut some shorter layers from underneath to produce movement around your face and let light shine through.

Trim on the Cheap

If you're used to getting an expensive haircut, it's hard to switch to a bargain salon such as Supercuts. But what you can do to save yourself hundreds of dollars a year is to get a hairstyle that doesn't need a lot of upkeep. When you need a trim in between cuts, go to an inexpensive salon. While hair stylists at the bargain salons sometimes can't give you the fancy cut you want, they can usually handle a simple trim, following the path of your normal stylist. If you just need your bangs cut, ask at your usual salon if they offer free bang trims in between cuts.

Stylists in Progress

Get your haircut on the cheap by students who are studying to be beauticians. You may risk a less-than-professional 'do, but it's probably better than having a friend do it. Student haircuts are also great for kids, whose simple cuts are usually hard to screw up.

Bang Bang

The next time your daughter needs her bangs cut, don't go to a costly salon for a trim. Do it yourself! Just put a strip of Scotch tape onto her bangs to hold them in place. Step back to make sure the tape is on straight, and then snip away along its edge.

Chapter Three
Make-Up & Other Cosmetics

Keep Them in the Dark

Many forms of make-up are sensitive to the sun due to their preservatives. Make sure to keep your make-up away from the window to ensure it lasts as long as possible.

Two Are Better Than One

If your eyeliner or lip pencils are too long for your make-up case, break them in half to form two smaller pencils and sharpen them both. You'll not only save space, but you'll have a backup if one pencil goes missing.

Cleaning Make-Up Brushes

Makeup brushes and sponges should be washed regularly to rid them of dirt, oil, and bacteria you don't want to transfer onto your face. Lather them up with baby shampoo, massage gently, and rinse in cool water. Let them air dry. You can also try this simple cleaning solvent: Combine ½ cup baking soda with 2 tablespoons water and mix together. Then add the resulting paste to one more cup of water and half a cup of fabric cleanser. Dip your brushes and sponges in the final solution, rinse clean, and reshape before allowing to air dry.

Brush-Up

Though we usually go with the cheapest option, when it comes to make-up brushes it's worth it to invest in high quality, and good brushes will make application easier, faster, and more polished-looking. Brushes should always have bristles that feel soft against the skin.

That Otherworldly Glow

How do those women get that otherworldly glow? You've tried all the bronzers and sun-kissed blush powders you can find, but can't seem to get that radiant skin. One trick is this: Apply a little bit of moisturizer *after* you apply your make-up.

Easy Radiance

When applying powder or bronzer to your face, start from your jawline and work your way in. Since you have more powder on the brush, your skin will looker darker where you begin, and having the darker shade on the outside will give your face a more radiant look.

Do It Up in the Daylight

When applying your make-up in the morning, always apply it under natural light, as your skin will look drastically different under the light from your bathroom bulb. Set up a magnifying mirror near a window with a good source of natural light, and make sure that shading is properly blended for the most natural-looking face.

Ditch a Double Chin

If a double chin is driving you nuts, use a little make-up to hide it. When applying powder or foundation to your face, use a slightly darker shade under your chin, which will make it appear to recede. Blend towards the back of the jawline to add definition. And when posing for pictures, stick your chin out as much as possible to stretch out the skin in the area.

Don't Be a Bag Lady

Partied a little too hard over the weekend? Don't make the mistake of covering up the bags under your eyes so dramatically that you draw attention to that spot by making it too light. A little bronzer applied over the concealer should even things out.

Tiny Purse? Tiny Powder!

You're headed out for a night on the town with that fantastic new clutch you found, but once you shove your cell phone, wallet, and keys in there you barely have room for your lipstick. So what do you do with the powder compact you were counting on for touch-ups? Simply take some of those pieces of pressed powder that inevitably break off of the mass and keep them in a tissue. When it's time to refresh, rub the tissue across your face.

Keeping It Light

Summer beauty requires a lighter touch. To keep your skin tone looking fresh and even, stash away your foundation and just use a tinted moisturizer with an SPF of 15 or higher to cover the occasional blemish and give protection from the sun.

Remove Redness After Waxing

When you get your eyebrows waxed, bring some eye drops with you. Applying a bit of the eye drops onto sensitive areas will reduce redness, allowing you to go to your waxing appointment and then back to the office!

Taming Unruly Brows

It's happened to the best of us: you look in the mirror and notice that your eyebrows are out of control! When this happens to you, a little dab of petroleum jelly—or even lip gloss in a pinch—can help keep curly hairs in a sleek, sophisticated line. Alternatively, use a little hair spray sprayed on your eyebrow brush to smooth them into place.

Know Your Brow Shape

Defining your brow line with a pencil and a little plucking is a great way to open up your face and make your eyes sparkle. But how do you know where your brows should begin and end? To determine exactly where your brow should begin, imagine a vertical line or hold a make-up pencil straight alongside one nostril. Where the pencil lands by your brow is where it should begin. To work out where the brow should end, imagine a line from the outside of your nostril to the outer corner of your eye, then extend it out to your brow.

Our Five Favorite
Hints for Long-Lasting Cosmetics

1. USE SPARINGLY
Most people use far more foundation than they need—and since it's one of the most expensive types of make-up, that's money down the drain! To make sure you're using the proper amount, simply apply one dot to each of your cheeks, your forehead, and your nose, then blend thoroughly. Don't be afraid to leave some areas bare.

2. STRETCH IT OUT
Spend less on your powder and foundation with this ingenious trick. Buy a shade darker than your natural shade, then mix it with baby powder (for powder) or moisturizer (for foundation) until it matches your normal color. You'll have more than twice as much, and you'll never be able to tell the difference!

3. PETROLEUM JELLY FOR PERFUME
Before putting on a splash of your favorite scent, rub a pit of petroleum jelly on your skin. It will keep your fragrance from fading.

4. LET LIPSTICK BIND
Dab some baby powder on your lips before applying lipstick. It will give the lipstick something to bind to, making multiple applications a thing of the past.

5. DITCH THE MAKE-UP REMOVER
For an inexpensive way to remove mascara, eye liner, and shadow, try baby shampoo. It contains many of the same ingredients as make-up remover, and works just as well. Dispense a small amount on a tissue or cotton ball, rub over closed eyes, and rinse with water.

Mascara Miracle

Applying the finishing touches to your make-up and realize you're out of mascara? Here's a great tip to get that last bit out of the tube. Simply roll the tube quickly between your hands for 30 seconds. The heat generated by the friction is enough to soften the mascara stuck to the sides of the tube, so you'll have just enough to apply to your lashes before you run out the door.

—KIM BRICKMAN, PEORIA, IL

Clumpy Mascara?

When your mascara starts to clump, you don't have to toss it out! Smooth it out again by letting the tube sit in a teacup of near-boiling water for five minutes.

For Fuller Lashes

To make your mascara last longer (and your lashes look fuller than ever), apply two coats every time you do your lashes. But here's the secret! In between the first and second coats, apply a thin layer of baby powder with a make-up brush. The mascara will adhere to the powder, making it stay on your lashes longer.

—JENNIFER RIVERA, INDIO, CA

Trick Lips

To give the illusion of a fuller upper lip, dab a tiny touch of pale, iridescent sheen in the center of the lips, then rub to blend in with the rest of your lipstick. This will highlight your cupid's bow (the curvy portion of your lips), making it appear bigger than it is.

Making Lipstick Last

After apply your lipstick, rub an ice cube over it. The cold will set the lipstick and prevent it from smudging and bleeding, especially on hot summer days.

Lip Tip

Avoid getting lipstick on your teeth. After you've applied lipstick, close your mouth over your finger and slowly pull it out. This will save you time and time again!

Make Your Teeth Look Whiter

Choose your lipstick color carefully! Shades of purple or blue-based pinks can make teeth look whiter, while orangey browns will make them look yellowish.

Our Five Favorite
Homemade Cuticle Creams

1. *ORANGE*
Mix 2 tablespoons each of olive oil and petroleum jelly along with the zest of half an orange. Store in the refrigerator, and apply at bedtime for soft, lovely-smelling nails.

2. *MAYONNAISE*
Believe it or not, mayonnaise is fantastic for your nail beds. Pour into a bowl and submerge your fingers. Keep in the fridge, but make sure nobody uses it on their sandwich!

3. *LEMON AND HONEY*
Mix together 2 parts lemon juice to one part honey and soak your fingers for 10 minutes. All you need is some tea!

4. *VEGETABLE OIL*
Simply rub a bit of vegetable oil into your cuticles every day after bathing. Your cuticles will never be softer!

5. *FANCY*
Whip together 1 tablespoon shea butter, 1 tablespoon cocoa butter, and 5 drops essential oil for a cuticle cream that's better than the pros'.

Strawberry Paste

An inexpensive (and all-natural) way to whiten your teeth is with strawberries! It's as simple as mashing up a few strawberries, and then applying the paste to your teeth after your usual brushing. (Just make sure no seeds get caught between your teeth!) Leave on for a few hours and the malic acid in the fruit will help lighten your teeth.

Boost Your Cleavage

If you're wearing a low-cut top, use a bit of powder to give your skin an even color and smooth appearance below your neck. Using a smidgen of blush down your cleavage line will add a "shadow," making your bust look a bit larger.

Don't Clown Around

I've used common vegetable oil to remove my make-up for years! It works better than anything else (even at removing waterproof mascara), is cheap, and is good for your skin. Take it from someone who used to be a mime and a clown!

—Bibi Caspari, Los Angeles, CA

Quick Make-Up Removal

You should never leave make-up on overnight, as it can dry out your skin (and leave marks on your pillow!). One of the quickest ways to remove make-up is with a pre-moistened wipe, but skip the expensive "make-up removal wipes" and keep of stash of baby wipes near the sink instead. The next time you come home after a late night, make sure to rub a wipe over your face before you hit the sack.

Too Much Perfume?

Oops! You accidentally put on way too much perfume, and you're afraid the restaurant you're going to will smell like someone just let off a flower-scented bomb! To make your perfume less strong but still a little fragrant, dab a bit of rubbing alcohol wherever you applied the scent with a cotton ball. Your friends will thank you!

Brighten Your Nails

Rub a wedge of lemon on your fingernails to whiten their enamel. This is a perfect activity for down-times while baking!

How 'Bout a Buff?

If your manicure usually ends up chipped, consider buffing your nails as an alternative. An expensive nail buffer can bring your nails to a natural shine that is sure to get noticed. Just make sure to only buff your nails once a week. Over-buffing weakens the nails by taking away their top layer and making them more porous.

Fast Dry for Nail Polish

You have just enough time to touch-up your nails before you leave—but not enough time to dry them. Make your nail polish dry more quickly by spraying your final coat with cooking spray. The oil will help them dry faster, and moisturize your cuticles, too!

Remove the Last of that Polish

If your fingernails have become stained by wearing dark nail polish, here's a quick fix: Plop a denture-cleaning tablet into a glass of water and soak your nails for a couple of minutes. The stain will come right off. This is also great for removing that last bit of old polish from your nails!

Never Pay Too Much for Make-Up

Thinking of switching brands to save on make-up? Choose one a good friend uses, and ask her if she'd be willing to buy it from you if you don't like it. That way, you know you won't be wasting your money if you don't like what you've bought.

Make-Up Must-Have

Most make-up is exactly the same, except for whether they call that shade of red you love "cherries jubilee" or "red crush." Make shopping for make-up easier by keeping an index card with your favorite colors on hand. Rub a bit of lipstick, blush, or eye shadow on the card, then mark down the brand and what the color is called. When it's time for more make-up, you can easily compare the colors of the sale brand with your card. Then write down what *that* color is called on your card. You'll soon have a list of all your favorite colors from each brand.

—ARLENE DeSANTOS

***

Chapter Four

Clothes & Accessories

Uplift Your Look

One of the narrowest areas on a woman's body is across the ribs, just beneath the bustline, yet large or droopy breasts can hide this area. Make your figure look more like an hourglass by wearing a supportive, push-up style bra, which will help make the line from rib to hip look more elongated and shapely.

Two-Minute Slimdown

You don't need to purchase a shaper and certainly not a corset to make yourself look five pounds slimmer. Try leotards, tight-fitting tank tops, leggings, and spandex running pants. The trick is to layer them underneath your nice outfit so you don't get the "Are those pajamas you're wearing?" look. You'll feel firmed up and pulled-together, at least until you catch sight of your hair.

Tummy Trick

Most of us have a little more tummy than we'd like. Luckily, you can help disguise it with the help of tailored pants. When shopping for dress pants, choose a look that has a flat front and a side zipper, which won't add any bulk to your front.

Embrace Your Curves

If you're not thin, you've been cursed to disfavorably compare yourself to movie stars for the rest of your life. The good news is that you also have curves that those women would kill for. Celebrate your womanly body by wearing clothes that show it off by hugging your sides. Wrap dresses and fitted clothes are always preferable to baggy clothing, which just hangs from your widest point and does nothing to show off your good points (and everybody has at least one good point)!

Play Up Your Best Features

The whole point of jewelry is to enhance your beauty. So if you're self-conscious about your neckline, by all means steer clear of a dramatic choker. Try bracelets and elegant headbands instead. If those daily crunches are starting to pay off, wear a flashy belt or bright scarf wrapped around just above the hips to draw attention to your slimming waistline.

She's Got Legs

Add a little extra length to your legs by always wearing pants that cover the top of your shoes and just skim the floor.

Single-Breasted Suits Us

As gravity (and middle-age) takes its toll, a layer of fat may be making its way around your midsection. We'll let you decide whether to hit the gym, but when you hit the store, stay away from double-breasted jackets. Always choose single-breasted suits, as two sets of buttons make the body appear wider.

The Kids May Be Onto Something

You may scoff that low-waisted pants are for teenagers only, but they can have their benefits. Jeans and pants that sit between the hips and the waist can help hide extra weight, as higher-waisted pants clamp the middle tummy, making it appear larger and highlighting a lack of waist.

Keep It Simple

When you're buying clothes, always go for classic looks rather than modern, stylized ones. A blue V-neck T-shirt will be fashionable year after year, while something with more exotic colors or patterns will go out of style quickly. Buying more basic clothing will make sure you don't have to buy as many new articles of clothing each season.

Begin in the (Bargain) Basement

How many times have you purchased an $80 sweater, only to find a nearly identical one for much less later? When you begin to look for clothes for the new season, always start at the least expensive store first. Since most clothing stores carry similar items each season, you'll make sure to get each piece for the best price. You should also try to buy most of your basics—solid-color T-shirts, socks, and so forth—at the cheaper stores. Save the expensive stores for the uniquely designed and patterned clothes, where you can see the difference in quality.

Befriend Those in the Know

If you have a favorite shop you find yourself spending a lot of time in, make sure to get friendly with the sales staff! Clothing stores often have unannounced sales, but if you're down with the people that work there, they'll often tip you off. And if they really like you, they may let you put an item on layaway until it goes on sale a few days later.

Our Five Favorite
Ways to Keep Clothes Lasting Longer

1. *WEAR THEM SEVERAL TIMES BEFORE WASHING*
Many of your clothes can be worn several times before you wash them, especially sweaters. Most items get more wear and tear from being in the washing machine than they do on your bodies, so it's worth it to keep them out of the washer.

2. *BE CAREFUL WITH KNITS AND DESIGNS*
Turn knitted clothes and T-shirts with designs on them inside-out when washing and drying.

3. *DON'T LET STAIN REMOVER SIT*
When pre-treating a stain, try to wash the item within an hour after applying the stain remover and it will be less strain on the fabric.

4. *IRON WISELY*
When ironing clothes, especially dark ones, turn them inside-out. Make sure to use distilled water if you use a steaming iron to prevent stains.

5. *LINE (OR TREE) DRY*
Not only is air-drying less harsh on your clothes, you'll love the real smell of sun-dried linens. If you don't have a clothes line, hang shirts and pants on hangers on tree limbs! Just make sure not to put brights in the sun, as they made fade.

Washing Delicates

Washing your delicate laundry doesn't have to be expensive. Just fill your bathroom sink with warm water and add ½ cup baking soda for every ½ cup water. The baking soda will wash the fabric without damaging it, at a very low price!

Hand-Washing Tip

When you're hand-washing cashmere and wool, add a drop of baby oil to the water during your last rinse. The oil will make the fabric more pliable, so you can more easily move it back into its original shape for drying.

—CECE BARRINGTON, SHELBY, NB

Keep Clothes Color-Fast

The secret ingredient to keeping your clothes from bleeding in the washing machine may surprise you—it's pepper! Throw a teaspoon of ground pepper into the washing machine with your dirty clothes and they'll be less likely to bleed and more likely to keep their bright colors longer.

The New Jeans Cure

Every time we get a new pair of jeans, we wash them in white vinegar mixed with water. Why? It will remove their stiffness and make sure they stay color-fast. Just throw them in the wash with 10 fluid ounces of vinegar and your usual amount of soap. And feel free to add other clothes, too! Vinegar is great for your wash.

Brighten Your Whites

Add ½ cup lemon juice to the wash cycle of your washing machine to brighten your white clothes. They'll also smell wonderful!

Get Rid of White Marks

You're getting ready for work, and you just realized your deodorant left a white streak on your blouse. The secret to removing these frustrating stains is simple: Just apply white vinegar! (Test a small area to make sure it's safe for the fabric first.) The vinegar will loosen the aluminum chloride in the deodorant, allowing you to more easily wipe it off.

Lipstick on Your Collar?

Lipstick prints on silk seem like disaster, but it's almost as easy to lift them off as it is to get them on there. Use transparent or masking tape to pull off the stain. Any remnants can be sprinkled with talcum powder and shaken off.

Tea Stains

Tea and lemon are best friends—even in the laundry room. Rub a tea stain with equal parts lemon juice and water. Just make sure the mixture only gets on the stain, using a Q-tip or eyedropper if necessary.

A Cup of Coffee Does the Trick

If your black cotton items are starting to look more like they're dark blue, wash a load of only black items. But first, brew a strong pot of black coffee, then add it to the rinse cycle.

When Stains Are The Pits

You don't have to throw out shirts with embarrassing yellow stains under the arms. Mix 2 tablespoons salt with 2 cups hot water and use a little elbow grease to rub the stain out.

Gummy Mess

If you've gotten gum on your clothes, try rubbing them with egg whites using an old toothbrush. If that doesn't work, you can also try placing a piece of wax paper on the affected area, then ironing the wax paper. The gum should transfer from the cloth to the paper—problem solved!

Water to the Rescue

To get juice stains off of your clothes, just use boiling water. Hold the garment over the tub and very carefully pour boiling water through the fabric where the stain is. It will remove the stain without having to put your clothes through the hot cycle in the washing machine.

—Chrys Garito, Bayonne, NJ

Help Sweaters Stay in Shape

Be careful when drying sweaters! Common laundry advice, but it usually stops there. You can't throw them in the dryer. You can't let them hang and fall out of shape. So what *are* you supposed to do? Once pantyhose have lost their shape, run the legs through the arms of your sweater so the waist is up at the sweater's neck. Use a hanger with clips to grab the ends of the pantyhose (the feet) and hang.

The Sweater Solution

Are the cuffs of your favorite sweater starting to get stretched out? Make them like new again by blowing them with hot air from your hairdryer! Just wet the cuffs with water, then set the hairdryer on its highest setting, then blow dry until no longer wet. The heat will shrink the cuffs slightly, bringing them back down to the right size.

—CHRISSIE BLUTE, DULUTH, MN

A Shave for Your Sweater

Next time you replace your disposable razor, keep the old one. Gently "shaving" your sweater will quickly and easily get rid of pills and lint.

Cedar to the Rescue

Clothes moths are a pain in the neck to get rid of once they've invaded your closets. Since mothballs are toxic, pick up cedar chips at a craft store instead—cedar is an effective and safe moth repellent. Stick the chips in cheesecloth or an old nylon sock, tie it closed, and store in closets or drawers to keep the pests away.

Storing Sweaters

When putting away your sweaters for the spring and summer months, wrap them in newspaper and tape the sides. The newspaper will keep away both moths and moisture.

Storing Leather and Suede

When storing leather and suede garments, don't cover them in plastic. These materials need a little breathing space, or they'll quickly dry out.

The Zipper Fix

Got a zipper that won't stay closed? Spray it lightly and carefully with hair spray after zipping up.

Our Five Favorite
Ironing Tips

1. VINEGAR: YOUR IRON'S BEST FRIEND

When ironing, mix one part white vinegar and one part water in a spray bottle. Use it on your garment to help remove iron-made creases (or make creases where you want them). This vinegar and water solution will also remove any shiny areas on the fabric caused by the hot iron.

2. STICKY IRON?

Get rid of unwanted residue on the bottom of your iron by sprinkling salt on a piece of printer paper and ironing on a low level with no steam.

3. QUICKER IRONING

Covering your ironing board with foil (shiny side up) before you iron your clothes will get them unwrinkled twice as fast, saving you time and energy!

4. UNCLOG YOUR STEAM IRON

If your iron is having trouble steaming, it's vinegar to the rescue again! Pour a little vinegar into the water chamber and turn the dial to "steam." Leave it upright for five minutes, then unplug and let the iron cool down. Any loose particles should fall out when you empty the water chamber.

5. GO FLAT

To quickly and easily iron the spaces between buttons on a shirt, use a flat iron that you would normally use for hair. (It's also a great way to rationalize buying another hair gadget!)

Hangin' Tough

Hang your blazers and suit jackets properly to save yourself trips to the cleaners for pressing. If you use wooden hangers, turn them so the curve is facing you when you slip the jacket or blazer around the shoulders, with the blazer also facing you. The hanger will be backward, and this method will keep the jacket's shoulders nice, tight, and wrinkle-free.

Fix a Slipping Shirt

If you have wide-necked shirts or other clothes that refuse to stay on hangers, enlist the help of some rubber bands. Just wrap them around the ends of hangers vertically, and the cloth of the shirt will "grab" onto their non-slip surface.

—JANICE LIPSCOMB

No-Wrinkle Packing Technique

When packing for vacation, place your pants in the bottom of the suitcase, with half of them hanging over the side. Place the rest of your clothes on top, then fold the pants back over on top of the clothes. When you unpack, your pants won't need to be pressed.

Bras That Don't Bust

Rotate through your bras rather than wear one for a few days in a row. You'll give the elastic time to contract and the bras will last longer. Who knew?

Prevent Pantyhose Runs

Weird but true: Freezing pantyhose can keep them from running. Before wearing a pair of nylons for the first time, stick them in the freezer overnight. The cold strengthens the fibers, which will keep them from running. Alternately, try soaking them in salty water before you wash and wear them. Use a half a cup of salt for each quart of water, and let them soak for 30 minutes. Then launder as usual.

No Wire Hangers, Ever?

One easy way to remove static cling is to run the long part of a wire hanger over the garment. If you've suffered any skirt-stuck-to-pantyhose embarrassment, run the hanger between your skirt and the pantyhose. Shape the hanger to fit inside pant legs or under a dress or skirt.

Static Trick

To get rid of static cling in a pinch, spray hair spray on the underside of your skirt or dress and, bada-bing, no more static cling.

—Jennee Busby, Bakersfield, CA

Need to Iron a Straw Hat?

Rescue a straw hat by placing a damp cloth between the straw and a warm iron. Rest the brim underside up on the ironing board and press, rotating the hat. For flat tops, place cardboard inside and pack with crumpled newspaper before pressing.

Clinging Cure

Slinky skirt grabbing your pantyhose and won't let go? Solve this annoyance with an unlikely household hero: a battery! Just rub the positive end of a battery over your skirt and hose. (If this happens to you a lot, you can just keep a AAA battery in your purse!) The battery releases positively charged ions that neutralize the negative ones that cause static cling.

Shiny Pearls for Life

Pearl buttons, whether they're real or fake, can benefit from a coating of clear nail polish. They'll be sturdier and shinier!

Button Business

Dab a small drop of clear nail polish on the front of a button to keep the threads in place and never lose a button again.

Baseball Cap Cleanse

Wash a baseball cap on the top rack of your dishwasher, and remove while still wet. Then, place the cap over a bowl to regain its shape, and dry it away from direct sunlight.

Iron On Your Favorite Fragrance

This smart tip will make your clothes smell wonderful. Add a drop of perfume to the water in your steam iron, then iron your shirts, underwear, lingerie—everything! You'll enjoy your favorite perfume wherever you go.

Our Five Favorite
DIY Earring Organizers

1. REPURPOSE A PRETTY FRAME

Make your own earring organizer with a piece of vinyl screen from a home supply store. First find an unused picture frame and remove the glass and cardboard backing. Cut the screen to fit inside your frame, and secure it in place. Hang earrings in the screen to keep them safe and organized.

2. GREAT USE FOR OLD BUTTONS

Here's an easy way to keep your earrings together: Thread the posts through old buttons, and then attach the backs.

3. GO DRINK SOME WINE

Corks are great for storing and toting stud earrings. Cut the cork into thin slices, then poke the earrings through, put the backs back on, and toss them into your toiletry bag when traveling.

4. GET CRAFTY

A shoebox lid makes a perfectly good organizer for your stud earrings. Just push them through and fasten the backs! Cover the lid with wrapping paper to make it part of your décor!

5. ORGANIZATION AWAITS!

Use cork in a different way by using a bulletin board to organize your dangly earrings. Hang them from thumb-tacks and they're easy to re-arrange and see all at one time to give you a whole different look at your earring wardrobe.

Keeping Lace Lovely

Nervous about ironing lace items? Don't be. Before ironing, simply dip the lace in sugar water, and your item should emerge from ironing unscathed.

How to Wash Lace

Even if you hand-wash it, lace can get easily tangled and torn when cleaning. To prevent this from happening, safety-pin the lace to a sheet or smaller cloth. Wash gently as usual, then unpin when dry.

Steam Away Smoke

To remove a smoky smell from your clothes, fill your bathtub with hot water and add 1 cup white vinegar. Then just hang the clothes above the steaming water, and the smoke smell will dissipate in about an half hour. Ah, vinegar—is there anything it can't do?

Restore Worn Velvet

If your velvet dress, shawl, shirt, or pants are getting a shiny mark from too much wear, you may be able to remove it. Try lightly spraying the area with water, then rubbing it against the grain with an old toothbrush.

Bird Got Your Leather?

If you were enjoying a nice day outside until a bird pooped on your leather jacket, don't go get your BB gun. Instead, rub a bit of petroleum jelly into the spot and let set for five minutes. It should rub right off.

A Facelift for Leather

Give a leather jacket a new lease on life! It's as easy as going to your kitchen cupboard and getting some olive oil. Rub the olive oil into your clean jacket with a soft cloth and your leather will never look and feel more supple.

Make Mending Easier

If you're mending a hole on a sleeve or pant leg, it's easy to miss a stitch when the fabric gets all balled up. Make your job easier by rolling up a magazine and placing it inside. It will partially unroll as far as the sleeve or leg will let it, creating just enough tension to hold the fabric in place.

The Trick for New Shoes

Cobblers will stretch out your new shoes for you, but there's no need to pay their price. Do it yourself by wearing your new shoes around the house and out to run errands for a few days, and wear two pairs of thick socks with them. The extra padding will stretch out the shoes until there is plenty of room for your feet, and will also make your feet less likely to get blisters when you're ready to wear your new shoes out on the town.

—BETSY BEIER, VIROQUA, WI

Slip-Proof Your Shoes

Going out in new shoes? Lots of fun. Slipping as you walk past your new crush? Not so much. Use sandpaper to distress slippery leather soles and slick surfaces won't slip you up.

Caring for Leather Shoes

New leather shoes? To wear them in without the blisters (OK, at least fewer blisters!), rub alcohol in at the heels and wear them while they're still wet. The alcohol will help stretch out the leather.

Leather Saver

It turns out that getting salt stains or on your "good leather shoes" is not the calamity you might have thought it was. You can easily get rid of stains and bring back the original luster of leather shoes and bags with shampoo. Rub it in with a soft cloth and then rinse with a damp one. To protect your shoes from getting damaged and stained by too salt in the first place, coat them with hair conditioner and let it soak in. The conditioner will repel the salt, and help keep leather shoes supple.

White Sneakers That Stay White

After purchasing new cotton sneakers, spray them with spray starch to help them resist stains. The starch will repel grease and dirt, keeping them whiter!

A Different Kind of Tar Heel

Is there anything worse than getting tar stuck to the bottom of your sneakers after walking across a hot street in the summer? Quickly get rid of the tar—even in the tiniest grooves—by applying some petroleum jelly. The jelly will bind to the tar and help it wipe right off.

Shoelace Trick

Having trouble keeping your (or your kids') shoelaces tied? Shoelaces are more likely to stay tied if you dampen them with water first.

Reboot Your Boots

Keep your boots looking their best by storing them with empty wine or soda bottles inside. It will keep your boots upright and help them maintain their shapes.

Been Out in the Rain?

You should never attempt to dry your shoes with a hairdryer, as the heat can make the rubber in the shoes soft and allow your shoes to become deformed. If you need dry shoes fast, use the blower end of a vacuum cleaner hose instead.

Dancin' Feet

Feet tend to swell. So after a long day of work, when you're getting ready to go out dancing with the girls, it can be a real tight squeeze to get into your favorite pumps. Rub your favorite lotion on your feet to help you slide in with ease.

Let Your Feet Breathe

It's tempting to buy the smallest pair of shoes your feet can fit into, but too-tight shoes can cause corns, calluses, bunions, and—later on down the line—bone spurs and hammer toe. Make sure your shoes are the right size, and if possible, don't wear the same pair of shoes two days in a row.

Freshen Feet

Stinky feet? Keep them fresh by sprinkling a bit of cornstarch into your shoes once or twice a week. The cornstarch will absorb moisture and odors, making you unafraid to slip off those uncomfortable dress shoes under your desk.

Daily Shoe Freshener

Another easy way to keep your shoes fresh is simply by storing a fabric softener sheet inside of them each night. They'll neutralize odors while you sleep.

Our Five Favorite
Ways to Polish Shoes

1. BANANAS
Instead of slipping on banana peels, use them to polish leather shoes. Rub the insides on your shoes, then buff for an especially finished look.

2. POTATOES
Scuff marks on your shoes can be removed with the help a potato! Just wipe the areas with the cut edge of a raw potato, then buff with a soft cloth.

3. LIP BALM
Scuffed your leather shoes on the way to dinner? Grab a bit of lip balm and rub a dab into your shoes, then buff with a tissue or piece of toilet paper. They'll look as good as new, even if they smell a bit like your favorite Chapstick!

4. COOKING OIL
When it comes to shining leather shoes, forget about expensive shoe polish. First, dampen a cloth and wipe away any dirt, then put a few drops of vegetable or olive oil on a clean, soft cloth and rub into your shoes. They'll shine like new!

5. HAIR SPRAY
When you're polishing your shoes, spray them with a bit of hair spray. People will wonder how you got them so shiny!

Twine Time

If you have a pair of espadrilles whose heels are looking ragged, patch them up with everyday brown twine you can find at the hardware store. Cut the twine into pieces that fit in the gaps and adhere with shoe glue.

Jewel-Polishing Potions

Wondering how to keep your beautiful jewelry looking like the first day you wore it? Gentle dishwashing detergent and water plus a soft cloth can clean rubies, amethysts, citrines, sapphires, and garnets. Emeralds are softer than other precious stones and can chip easily. Wash each piece by itself carefully in a warm solution of water and dishwashing liquid. To take care of diamonds, fill a small pot with a cup of water, plus a teaspoon of dishwasher detergent. Add your diamonds, bring the water to a boil, then turn off the heat and let the pot sit until it cools. Once it's cool (and not before), carefully remove your jewelry and rinse.

Join the Club

Emeralds, diamonds, rubies, and sapphires can also be washed with club soda. Place them in a glass of it overnight, and they will shine like new in the morning.

More Tips for Gem Care

Since turquoise and opals are porous stones, never immerse them in water. Instead, polish them with a soft, dry chamois, and clean claws with a soft bristle brush. Bring back the magic of marcasite by polishing it with a soft brush and then buffing with a chamois—it should never be washed. Wipe amber with a soft cloth wrung out in warm, soapy water. Dry at once (water makes amber cloudy), and wipe with sweet almond oil to remove any grease marks.

Prescription for Pearls

The best way to care for a pearl (or coral) necklace is to wear it regularly—oils from your skin add a gentle luster. After wearing, wipe with a chamois to remove traces of perspiration that can damage the surface.

A Pool No-No

Never wear silver jewelry in pools, because chlorine can cause pitting, small indentations in the surface. It's not a particularly good idea to wear gold jewelry in chlorinated water either, so make sure to leave your valuables at home before heading to the pool.

Science Experiment

If your silver jewelry is starting to look a little dull or needs polishing, stick it in a bowl with a few tablespoons of baking soda and a square of aluminum foil. Let it sit for about 30 minutes, then wipe clean. The aluminum acts as a catalyst for ion exchange, a process that will make the tarnish transfer from your silver to the salt bath. This is the magic of science, folks!

—BROOKE LLEWELLYN, KANSAS CITY, MO

DIY Necklace Holders

You don't have to buy a jewelry organizer to keep your necklaces untangled. Just cut plastic straws in half, thread your necklaces through, and fasten the clasps. They'll never tangle again!

What a Relief It Is

Costume or inexpensive jewelry can be cleaned by dropping two Alka Seltzer tablets into a glass of water. Immerse for about five minutes and pat dry with a clean towel.

Good as Gold

Here's the recipe that my mother always used to wash her gold jewelry: Mix 1 teaspoon dishwashing liquid with ½ teaspoon ammonia and 1 cup warm water. Dip the jewelry into the solution for 10 seconds, and use an old toothbrush to brush off any marks. Your gold will look sparkling new!

—PHOEBE SMALLS, BURBANK, CA

Pearl of Wisdom

It's great to organize necklaces by hanging them—all except pearls. These gems are strung on a delicate silk thread that can't sustain the weight. Who knew?

Ring Trick

If you are unable to remove a ring from your finger, run your hands under very cold water for a few seconds. The cold will make your blood vessels (and, in turn, your finger) a little bit smaller, allowing you to slip off the ring. For a really stubborn situation, go the messier route—rub baby or olive oil over the area for a little lubrication.

Fix Broken Jewelry

If a stone has popped out a piece of your jewelry and you were lucky enough to save it, you can easily put it back in place with a tiny dab of clear nail polish.

Untangling Necklaces

For annoying tangles in thin chains, place on a glass surface. Add a drop of oil and use a pin to tease out the knots. Then rinse in warm water.

Remove Water from Your Watch

If you've ever seen condensation under your watch face, you know how frustrating it can be! Luckily, there's a solution. Simply strap the watch to a light bulb and turn it on for a few minutes. The heat from the bulb is the perfect amount to make the water disappear.

Quick Bracelet Fastening

Having trouble getting that bracelet on? Make fastening easy by attaching the bracelet to your arm with a bit of tape. Then, clasp, pull the tape off, and go!

Keep Necklaces Safe

Packing for a trip? Keep your necklaces safe and tangle-free by taping them to some bubble wrap. Then roll the wrap up and pack safely in your suitcase.

Jewelry On-the-Go

Repurpose a plastic daily vitamin/pill container into a jewelry container that's perfect for trips. Rings, earrings, and even necklaces fit perfectly inside, and it will make sure you're accessorized for each day you're away!

Impromptu Glasses Cleaner

The next time you're digging through your pockets looking for a cloth you can clean your glasses with, try a dollar bill. Press hard and it will do the job of a glasses cloth in a pinch.

Toothpaste Trick

Most optometrists will try to sell you an expensive cleaner when you buy your glasses. Instead of buying theirs, simply use a tiny dab of white toothpaste (not a gel) on both sides of the lenses to polish them and keep them from fogging up.

Too Much Hair Spray?

If you've gotten hair spray on your eyeglasses, just wipe them down with rubbing alcohol and you'll be seeing clearly again.

Twist Their Arms

If your sunglasses have gotten completely twisted, don't throw them out. Just turn a blow-dryer on high and aim it at your frames. The heat makes the plastic arms flexible enough that you should be able to gently bend them into their original shape.

Chapter Five

Natural Remedies & First Aid

Longer Than Big Red

Bad breath? Eat some yogurt! The "good" bacteria in yogurt has been found to be effective in targeting the odor-causing bacteria in your mouth. Make sure you go for the plain kind without sugar. Breath mints and sprays mask the odor but they don't help the underlying problem—eating yogurt does.

Surprising Use for a Coffee Bean

For a super quick way to freshen your breath, try sucking on a coffee bean. It's much cheaper than a breath mint, and tastes great to us coffee addicts!

Great Breath Fast

You don't need expensive mouthwashes to get better breath. Simply gargle with a mixture of 1 cup water, ½ teaspoon baking soda, and ½ teaspoon salt. This combo will knock out any germs that are causing your bad breath.

Say Cheese

Serve hard cheese like Romano and aged Cheddar as an after-dinner snack. They'll help scrub your teeth of acids found in other foods, and the calcium inside helps make teeth stronger.

Water, Water, Everywhere

How much water is enough water? Divide you body weight in half. The number you come up with is how many ounces of water you should be drinking daily. For example, if you weigh 150 pounds, you should consume 75 ounces of water each day.

Pepper Your Dishes

Why not use a sprinkling of cayenne pepper to help season your sauces? Derived from the plant *Capsicum annuum*, it has been reported to not only make you lose weight by elevating body temperature, but to improve circulation and to lower cholesterol. As it's a mild stimulant, it can also be added to hot water with lemon juice as an alternative to coffee.

Sage Advice

To cut down on how much you perspire, try drinking sage tea. Herbalists say it will take several weeks, but you'll see results!

Avoid Insulin Surge

Caffeine on an empty stomach stimulates insulin surge, which leads to unbalanced blood sugar and weight gain, in addition to taxing your adrenal glands. Instead of drinking coffee first thing in the morning, try having it with your afternoon snack—or at least after you've had breakfast.

Choose Your Carbs Wisely

It's hard to resist taking something from the bread basket when you're out to eat. But if you're looking to lose weight (or just maintain it), choose a hard roll, a piece of French or Italian bread, a wafer, pita bread, or melba toast. These don't have as much butter or sugar as soft rolls, breadsticks, biscuits, croissants, and muffins.

Detox with Lemon

Lemon juice not only smells great, it tastes delicious, too. Mix it with hot water and try it as an alternative to hot tea and coffee. You may find it wakes you up just as well, and your body will thank you.

Kick Your Sweet Tooth's Habit

Here are two quick tricks to eliminate the craving for sweets (without hitting the fridge). One way is to place a small amount of salt on your tongue and let it slowly dissolve. The second: Dissolve about a teaspoon of baking soda in a glass of warm water, then rinse your mouth out and spit (don't swallow). The salt or baking soda tends to stimulate the production of saliva, which eliminates your sweet craving.

Grape Expectations

Tried everything but you can't defeat your sweet tooth? Keep a bunch of grapes in your fridge and grab a handful when the hunger hits. Grapes release sugar quickly, so they are great for satisfying that sugar craving.

Our Five Favorite
Unusual Uses for Tea

1. SOOTHE SORE GUMS

A cool, damp tea bag can soothe aching gums from lost or new teeth. Hold the tea bag on the affected area, but don't bite through.

2. CURE POISON IVY

Tea can help dry up weepy poison ivy blisters. Strongly brewed tea works best, so leave the bags in for at least five minutes. Use a cotton ball to apply and allow to air-dry.

3. RELIEVE RAZOR BURN

Bring your morning cup of tea in with you when you shave. A wet tea bag will offer immediate relief when applied to razor cuts or burns.

4. REVITALIZE DULL HAIR

If you're tired of sticky conditioners that leave your hair feeling not-so-squeaky-clean, try this: Rinse with a teapot full of tea. It should be warm, not hot, freshly brewed with either tea bags or a mix. Cheap, fast, and refreshing.

5. CURE COLD SORES

The tannic acid in tea helps relieve inflammation, especially in cold sores. Place a used tea bag on the affected areas for 3 minutes. To make it feel even better, place the tea bag in the freezer for 10 minutes beforehand.

Guard Against Hair Loss

Thinning hair that falls out in clumps can come about as a result of a restricted diet. Hair loss from lack of vitamins B and C and iron can be rectified with a diet rich in protein and vegetables. Packed with EFAs (essential fatty acids), flax seeds will make hair thicker and shinier. If your hair has become weaker and more brittle with a tendency to break easily, try infusing rosemary in water and pour it over your hair after your final rinse. You can also massage some rosemary essential oil (mixed with baby oil) onto your scalp to help promote growth and strength.

Lutein for Healthy Eyes

Many people suffer from farsightedness, cataracts, glaucoma and other eye problems as they age. To keep your eyes healthy, increase your level of lutein—available in vegetables such as carrots, broccoli, spinach, Brussels sprouts and kale. Lutein can decrease the risk of cataracts and macular degeneration.

The All-Natural Prozac

The herbal supplement St. John's Wort can help ease feelings of depression and lift black moods. It is thought to increase the activity and prolong the action of the neurotransmitters serotonin and noradrenalin in a similar way to standard antidepressants, and will need to be taken for a few weeks before it starts working.

A Breath of Fresh Air

This is simple advice we've all heard before, but how often do we put it into practice? When you're feeling anxious or overwhelmed, take a deep breath. Take five, as a matter of fact. Start in your belly—envision blowing up a balloon there—and move to your chest, filling your lungs to their capacity. Exhale slowly. This is also a great method if you're having trouble falling asleep, since it signals to your nervous system that it's time to relax.

Furry Friends

Playing with or petting your pet is known to reduce blood pressure, improve your mood, and reduce stress. It been proven to work with all pets: dogs, cats, hamsters—everything but dust bunnies.

Relieve Stress in a Pinch

Many people hold stress in the area between their eyebrows, and in time, vertical stress lines will develop here. When you feel your brow knit together with concentration or stress, take a moment to pinch the muscle there, working from the center of the brow along the brow-line in each direction with a thumb and bent forefinger.

Wrinkle Cure and Face Massage in One

When you're feeling too lazy to hit the gym, work out your face instead! Doing facial exercises can help keep your skin looking fresh and young. Begin with this exercise for tired eyes: Simply look up and down with your eyes closed. Then move on to massaging your temples, which not only feels nice, but also helps relieve headache tension and can help prevent wrinkles. Pulling your skin from the eyebrows outward is also a good wrinkle-preventer. Exercise your cheeks by rubbing them in circles, chewing gum, and blowing on an instrument or into a straw.

Exercise the Easy Way

Claiming you're too busy to exercise is just an excuse! Start getting in shape *today* by using your stairs (if you have them) and cans of food as hand weights. You can march in place anywhere, do squats while waiting for the pasta to cook, and rotate your arms while talking on the phone with a headset. If you have some exercise equipment, but want access to more, try circuit training with a neighbor—you have a bike and treadmill, she has a weight machine and rower. Trade every other day. Even without any machines you can create your own little circuit, setting up stations to do sit-ups, push-ups, jumping jacks, and even a few yoga poses if you're feeling adventurous.

A Good, Stiff Drink

If you find you're often stiff after exercising, you probably just need more water. Dehydration is a major cause of post-exercise muscle soreness. Drinking water regularly while you work out should keep water levels high enough to combat pain.

Contrast Showers

You'll love the feeling of this simple routine that will help boost your immune and circulatory systems and even relieve stress. Toward the end of your shower, turn it up as hot as you can stand it and allow it to warm your body for three minutes. Then turn it down so the water is cool, and let it run over your body for 30–60 seconds. Repeat as many times as you like, ending on cold. When you get out of the shower, rub yourself vigorously with a towel to encourage circulation. Do not continue the contrasting temperatures, however, if you feel dizzy, nauseated, or excessively chilled.

Rx, Vinegar

White vinegar stops nosebleeds. Just dampen a cotton ball and plug the nostril. The acetic acid in the vinegar cauterizes the wound. Who knew?

Slippery Solution

Soothe and help heal minor bruises and scrapes by using the inside of a banana peel to gently rub the injury. Treat as fast as possible to reduce bruising.

Cures for Canker Sores

Hydrogen peroxide may help reduce and relieve canker sores. Simply mix one part peroxide with one part water, then dab on any affected areas several times a day or swish around in your mouth for as long as possible. If you feel a canker sore coming on but it hasn't erupted yet, hold a slice of fresh garlic to the spot for ten minutes. It'll make your breath stink but it will also stop the sore from forming.

Homemade Heating Pad

Don't spend your money on an aromatherapy pillow! Instead, add uncooked, long-grain rice to a sock and tie it shut. Whenever you need a little heat after a long day, stick it in the microwave on high for 1–2 minutes and you'll have soothing warmth. To add a little scent to the pillow, add a few drops of your favorite essential oil to the rice.

Toothpaste for Burns

If you've sustained a minor burn, cover it with white, non-gel toothpaste to ease the pain and help it heal.

Our Five Favorite
Insomnia Cures

1. *SALT SEDATION*
At bedtime drink a glass of water, then let a pinch of salt dissolve on your tongue. (Just make sure the salt doesn't touch the roof of your mouth). Studies show the combination of salt and water can induce a deep sleep.

2. *WARM BATH*
A warm bath not only feels great, it relaxes your muscles as promotes a "relaxation response" in your nervous system that will help get you ready for bed.

3. *YOUR CIRCADIAN RHYTHM*
From our days as hunter-gatherers, our adrenal glands are designed to start secreting energy-producing hormones when the sun rises. If you sleep when it's dark and rise with the sun, you're allowing your body to get rest at the times it expects to rest.

4. *NATURAL ELIXIR*
Blend up this juice, which contains natural sedatives called lactones: 3 apples, 2 oranges, 1 tablespoon lemon juice, and 2 handfuls iceberg lettuce. Drink before bed and you'll be sleeping in no time! Keep any extra in a sealed container in the fridge.

5. *THE DARK ROOM*
Up late watching TV? At least turn out the light. The absence of light on the skin encourages production of serotonin, a neurotransmitter that is vital for healthy sleep, and the hormone melatonin, which promotes deep sleep.

Tiny Ice Packs

Get rid of the hundreds of condiment packets in your junk drawer and help ease the pain of smaller bruises, scrapes, and burns by keeping the packets in your freezer, then taping them to bruises when injuries occur.

Try Honey, Honey

The ancient Egyptians relied on honey for cuts and burns long before antibiotics were around. Besides offering a soothing protective layer over minor wounds, the honey provides a natural antibiotic. Put a layer of pure honey on before a bandage.

Sanitize a Cut

You just got a nasty cut on your hand, but don't have anything to clean it out with before you put the bandage on. Luckily, there's something in your medicine cabinet that you may not have thought of—mouthwash. The alcohol-based formula for mouthwash was originally used as an antiseptic during surgeries, so it will definitely work for your cut, too.

Splinter Removal

Splinters used to be major events at our house until we discovered this trick: Vegetable oil softens the skin and helps the offending piece of wood slide back out. You can also put a drop of white glue over the offending piece of wood, let it dry, and then peel off the dried glue. The splinter will stick to the glue and come right out.

Keeping Finger Bandages Dry

You put a Band-Aid on your finger to cover up a scratch, but you still have to go through your day full of hand-washing, child-bathing, and dishes-doing. To keep the bandage dry while you work, cover it with a non-inflated balloon—any color will do!

PB&B

The blisters are gone but the Band-Aid tracks remain. Use peanut butter to get rid of the black marks and stop distracting everyone from your lovely pedicure!

Be Callous to Calluses

Get rid of ugly, unwanted calluses by dabbing them with chest rub, then covering them with bandages and leaving overnight. Repeat this procedure several days in a row and your calluses will disappear in no time. Believe or not, chest rub is also good for curing toenail fungus!

Another Callus Cure

To remove hard calluses from your feet, try this old-fashioned but effective remedy: Grind a few aspirin tablets into a paste with equal parts lemon juice and water. Apply it to the calluses, then wrap your feet in a hot towel, cover in plastic bags, and stay off your feet for 30 minutes. When you unwrap your feet, the calluses will be soft and ready to be filed off with a nail file or pumice stone.

Bee Careful

If you're stung by a bee, carefully grasp the stinger and pull it out as fast as you can. The less venom that enters your body, the smaller and less painful the resulting welt will be. Ice the area immediately to reduce the swelling. If it still hurts, try cutting an onion in half and applying the fleshy side to the sting. It should help ease the pain.

Duct Tape for Warts

It's long been stated as fact—then disputed—that duct tape can help cure warts. It may seem strange, but medical studies have concluded that when patients cover their warts with duct tape every day for a months, 85 percent of them will see a reduction in the wart. That's compared to only a 60 percent reduction in patients who used cryotherapy (having the wart frozen off by a dermatologist). It's hard to believe, but many people swear by the treatment! Our opinion? Especially if you don't have health insurance, it's worth a shot.

Help for Stings

Believe it or not, meat tenderizer works wonders on all sorts of stings—bee, wasp, even jellyfish. That's because it contains papain, which helps break down the proteins in venom. Make a paste with the tenderizer by adding a few drops of water at a time, then rub on the affected area.

Our Five Favorite
Medicinal Uses
for Vinegar

1. HELP BURNED SKIN
To help ease the pain of a minor burn, rub vinegar on the affected area with a cotton ball or soft cloth. It may smell a bit like salad dressing, but your skin will immediately feel cooler.

2. GET RID OF SWIMMER'S EAR
If your children are prone to swimmer's ear, a bacterial infection of the ear canal, take this precaution when they've been in the pool: Dab a solution of one part vinegar and five parts warm water into each ear three times a day. The vinegar will ward off bacteria and keep your kids' ears pain-free.

3. EASE WASP STINGS
Stung by a wasp? Apply apple cider vinegar to the area with a cotton ball and the sting will subside.

4. REMOVE CORNS
To get rid of corns, soak a Band-Aid in apple cider vinegar, and apply it to the corn for a day or two. You can also try soaking your feet in a shallow pan of warm water with half a cup of vinegar. Either way, finish by rubbing the corn with a clean pumice stone or old nail file (just don't use on your nails again).

5. SOOTHE BRUISES
Soak a cotton ball in white vinegar, then apply it to the bruise for an hour. It will reduce the blueness of the bruise and speed up the healing process.

Be Itch-Free

A great way to treat mosquito bites is with a dab of ammonia, which stops them from itching. In fact, ammonia is the main ingredient in many of the itch-relief products currently on the market. You can also try a dab of rubbing alcohol.

Getting Rid of Lice Naturally

Nothing strikes fear in the hearts of parents like the words "lice outbreak." The harsh chemicals that are used to fight lice are almost as bad as the lice themselves. Luckily, there is a cheaper, more natural alternative. Cover your child's head (or yours, if the little buggers have gotten you!) with a thick conditioner like Pantene Pro V. Put on a Disney movie to keep your kid busy, then get a fine-toothed metal comb. Dip the comb into rubbing alcohol and comb through the hair, staying close to the scalp. Between each swipe, wipe the comb on a white paper towel to make sure you're getting the lice. Dip the comb in the alcohol again and keep going. Cover the hair with baking soda, and then repeat the process with the alcohol and the comb. Wash hair thoroughly when finished, and repeat this procedure each day for a week or until the lice are gone.

Diaper Rash Ointment

When your baby gets diaper rash, nix those pricey ointments and try a homemade remedy instead. Make a paste with about ¼ cup petroleum jelly and 1 tablespoon cornstarch, then spread it along your baby's irritated skin. Also, try adding a cup of baking soda to your baby's bathwater.

Don't Horse Around with Aches

If you're suffering from aching muscles (either from illness or too much exercise), try this homemade cure. Mix 1 tablespoon horseradish with 1 cup olive oil. Let sit for 30 minutes, then apply it to aching areas.

Soothing Back Pain

If you have chronic back pain—especially associated with arthritis—or other sore muscles, try adding yellow mustard to a hot bath. Add a few tablespoons for mild pain, and up to a whole 8-ounce bottle if the pain is severe. The bathwater may look strange, but your aching back will thank you.

Aid Arthritis with Oatmeal

Believe it or not, you can help relieve arthritis pain with oatmeal. Just mix 2 cups oatmeal with 1 cup water, warm the mixture in the microwave, and apply to the affected area.

Poison Ivy?

To help relieve the itching of a rash caused by poison ivy, soak the affected area in a strong salt bath. Make sure the water is warm to fully get the itch out.

Help for an Stomach Ache

If your stomach is upset due to indigestion or a hangover, try drinking a glass of club soda with a dash of bitters. It should help ease your pain.

Rub Away the Bloat

Feeling bloated? It could just be trapped gas. Encourage it to move by gently stroking from your right hip up towards your ribs, then across the bottom of your ribcage and down towards your left hip. Repeat several times.

Relieve Nausea Naturally

Nothing's worse than a bad bout of nausea. Try this simple trick to help relieve your discomfort: Drink a little ginger ale, then chew a handful of crushed ice, and finally sniff a piece of black-and-white newspaper. It may seem like an old wives' tale, but it works!

Root Out Morning Sickness

Ginger root, taken as a powder or in tea, works directly in the gastrointestinal tract by interfering with the feedback mechanisms that send sickness messages to the brain. Take some when you're feeling nauseated to help alleviate your symptoms.

Stop Motion Sickness in Its Tracks

If you get nauseated every time you ride in a car, boat, or train, take some lemon wedges with you. Suck on them as you ride to relieve nausea.

Our Five Favorite
Ways to Halt Hiccups

1. LEMON JUICE

Just can't stop hiccupping? Swallow a tablespoon of lemon juice when holding your breath doesn't work. You can also put bitters on a lemon wedge and suck the juice from the wedge.

2. SUGAR

This treatment may make you *want* to get the hiccups! Put some sugar under your tongue and let it slowly dissolve.

3. Q-TIP

Insert a Q-tip into your mouth and gently dab the back of the throat under the soft palate. You'll stop hiccups immediately if you can hit your mouth's uvula (look it up, because you may need a diagram to help your aim!).

4. BUTTER KNIFE

It sounds strange, but we swear it's worked for us! Place a butter knife, blade up, into a full glass of water. Drink the water as quickly as possible with the cool knife blade resting on your forehead.

5. PICKLE JUICE

Old wives' tale or reality? Try it out and let us know: Drink a teaspoon of pickle juice every ten seconds to stop hiccups fast.

Sore Throat?

Aspirin does more than just relieve headaches! If you have a sore throat, dissolve two non-coated tablets in a glass of water and gargle. Just make sure to note that this only works with aspirin—don't try it with other pain relievers like ibuprofen.

Tasty Remedy

Relieve your sore throat with a time-tested home remedy. Slice one-third of a lemon off, then take the two-thirds-sized piece and place it on a shish kebab skewer or barbecue fork. Set your gas stove to high and roast the lemon over the open flame until the peel acquires a golden brown color. (This works on electric stoves too, although not quite as well.) Let the lemon cool off for a moment, then squeeze the juice into the smallest cup you have. Add one teaspoon of honey, mix well, and swallow.

Better than a Bloody Mary

In the peak of sore throat season, get a reprieve with this spicy mix: $1/3$ cup tomato juice, $1/2$ cup hot water, 5 drops pepper sauce. Gargle. It works even better if you gargle with lukewarm saltwater first. If you prefer sweet to salty, fill a shot glass with honey, then warm it in the microwave for about 10 seconds on high. Stir in $1/4$ teaspoon cinnamon, then drink.

Watery Eyes?

If your eyes are itchy, try this quick fix to cut down on your misery: Rub a small amount of baby shampoo on your eyelids. It should reduce your symptoms dramatically.

Scallion Cure

Stuffy nose? Don't spend money on decongestant—head to your fridge instead. Cut the "root" end of two scallions and carefully insert the white ends into your nose (being cautious not to shove them too high!). You may look silly, but your nose will start to clear in a couple of minutes.

Warming Socks

If you have a cold that's been hanging around forever, try this remedy to rid yourself of congestion once and for all. Get a pair of cotton socks damp, but not dripping, with cold water. You can even put them in the freezer for a couple minutes to make them extra cold. Put them on, and then put a pair of dry wool socks on over them. Go to bed immediately. As you sleep, the heat from your upper body will be drawn down to your feet, allowing the inflammation to reduce. You'll be stunned to find that your feet are warm and dry by morning.

Steam Away a Cold

Steam is a wonderful household remedy for colds, especially with some aromatherapy oils mixed in. Try pouring hot water into a bowl and breathing in as you lean over it. Stick your tongue out as you do it—this will open the throat and allow more steam through, which prevents membranes from drying out. Add aromatherapy oils to the water that are especially known to alleviate the symptoms of congestion, such as black pepper, eucalyptus, hyssop, pine, and sweet thyme.

Ancient Cold Relief

Ayurveda is a practice of natural medicine that's been used in India since around 1500 BC. Try this cold remedy that's been passed down through the ages: At the very first sign of a cold, mix 1 teaspoon water with 1 teaspoon raw honey and ½ teaspoon turmeric. Eat it every few hours until symptoms disappear.

Onion Ear Muffs

Oil found in raw onion is anti-microbial, which makes onions great cures for upper respiratory ailments. If you have a minor earache, onion may help. Slice a fresh onion and heat it in the microwave on High for one minute. Wrap it in cheesecloth or another thin cloth so that it doesn't burn your skin, and then hold it against the ailing ear for 20–30 minutes. See a doctor if the pain gets worse or continues for longer than 24 hours.

Get Rid of Headaches

An old-fashioned and effective way to treat headaches is to cut a lime in half and rub it on your forehead. In a few minutes, the throbbing should subside.

Are Your Eyes Causing Headaches?

Less-than-perfect eyesight can trigger headaches because the muscles around the eyes squeeze in order to focus. If your headaches come on after reading or working at a computer, make sure you give your eyes a rest every 15 minutes by focusing on a distant object for at least a minute. You may also want to get your eyes examined to see if you need glasses.

Drink Up

Many headaches are caused by dehydration. Before you reach for the pain reliever, try drinking two or three glasses of water or an energy drink like Gatorade. You may find you're back to normal in no time.

Headache Help

If your tend to get headaches in the late mornings, late afternoons, and after a long nap, they might be due to low blood sugar, also known as hypoglycemia. These headaches can be helped by eating foods that release sugar slowly, such as bananas, whole grains, and oats.

Hangover Cure

Party too hard last night? Just spread a little honey on your favorite crackers. The honey provides your body with the essential sodium, potassium, and fructose it needs after a raucous night out!

Alleviate Neck Tension

Been leaning over your work too long? Try this to help a hurting neck. Inhale and raise your shoulders up to your ears, pulling them as high as they will go. Then let go with an "ahhh" and drop them slowly back down. Repeat several times to release muscle tension.

Get Rid of Headaches

An old-fashioned and effective way to treat headaches is to cut a lime in half and rub it on your forehead. In a few minutes, the throbbing should subside.

Index

who knew?

online

Visit us on the web at WhoKnewTips.com!

* **Money-saving tips**
* **Quick 'n' easy recipes**
* **Who Knew? products**
* **And much more!**

Twitter.com/WhoKnewTips
Get a free daily tip and ask us your questions

YouTube.com/WhoKnewTips
Watch demos of your favorite tips

Facebook.com/WhoKnewTips
Daily tips, giveaways, and more fun!